© 2005 Mandragora. All rights reserved.

Mandragora s.r.l.
Piazza del Duomo 9, 50122 Firenze
www.mandragora.it

Edited, designed and typeset by
Monica Fintoni, Andrea Paoletti, Michèle Fantoli

Technical assistant
Paola Vannucchi

English translation by
Jeremy Carden

Photographs
Andrea Bazzechi, Florence; Paolo Busato, Florence;
Studio Lensini, Siena; Mandragora Archive

Printed in Italy by Alpilito, Florence

isbn 88-7461-033-5

This book is printed on TCF (totally chlorine free) paper.

Siena
Playing with Art

illustrations by Marta Manetti
text by Michèle Fantoli

Mandragora

1. Abracadabra! Hi there, my name's Martin. I'm a poet, musician, painter, dancer, knight, peasant. I'm even a jockey, juggler and tightrope walker.

How's that possible?
We're in Siena, you know, and I'm a little wizard!

2. Now listen carefully. I want to start by telling you about the famous legend of the founding of the city. See that she-wolf?

Everyone knows it's the symbol of Rome, but it's also one of the most important emblems of Siena. It arrived here together with the sons of Remus, Ascius and Senius, who are reckoned to have founded the city. The two brothers had escaped from Rome, where Uncle Romulus had just killed their father. Before they ran off, though, they pinched the she-wolf to spite their uncle.

3. Cities are usually built near water: by the sea, a river, a lake… But look, there's nothing like that here. Yet Siena does have its own river, the Diana: part goddess, part witch, but above all part phantom.

In fact, although no one is allowed to doubt its existence, it's never actually been seen! So the Sienese had to dream up ways of getting water to public fountains like Fontebranda and to countless private wells around the city. They did it by building an impressive underground aqueduct formed by a network of tunnels at least twenty-five kilometres long.

4. Around the year one thousand Siena was an important stopping-off point for pilgrims travelling to Rome along the Via Francigena. That's why they built a hospital, which is called Spedale di Santa Maria della Scala because it's in front of the steps (*scale*) leading up to the Cathedral. It was a left-luggage office, a shelter for pilgrims, but also a modern, well-equipped hospital,

with urine tests, care for the injured (though the patient here looks freezing—or is he just terrified?), confession for the dying, a cat, a dog…

5. If I don't start training now I'll never make it to the top of the Torre del Mangia—all 102 metres of it! By the way, who was 'il Mangia'? The architect? The builder? No! He was a 14th-century bell-ringer called Giovanni di Duccio, whose nickname was Mangiaguadagni ('Eat-the-profits'). He was later replaced by a mechanical device, which inherited not only the job but also the name.

6. Rich and powerful, in the 13th and 14th centuries Siena had to defend itself against its enemies. As was the custom in those days, the city relied on *condottieri*, the leaders of mercenary troops who sold their services to the highest bidder.

ANO·DNI·MCCCXXVIII

However, *condottieri* had
a high standing in society,
and leading painters often did
portraits of them in public
places. This, for instance,
is Guidoriccio da Fogliano
in the palace of the Comune.

7. The city government was also keen to sing its own praises on the walls of its palace. This is the *Effects of Good Government in the City and Countryside*, which illustrates the everyday life of the Sienese in the 14th century.

Then, of course, there are the wine shops and delis! And for anyone with a sweet tooth, remember that Siena is not only famous for its sausage meats and cheeses but also its sweets!

8. Hey! Look up!
I'm up here,
on the Cathedral
bell tower!
Isn't this giant zebra
towering over
the red roofs of Siena
just fantastic?

9. Yes, well, I've borrowed one of the lions from the pulpit. Poor things, they could do with someone to play with, they always look so serious… Understandable though— the pulpit they're propping up was used by the bishops of Siena!

They've got plenty of company: there are more than 300 characters and at least 70 animals on the seven panels of the parapet. Why don't you try counting them?

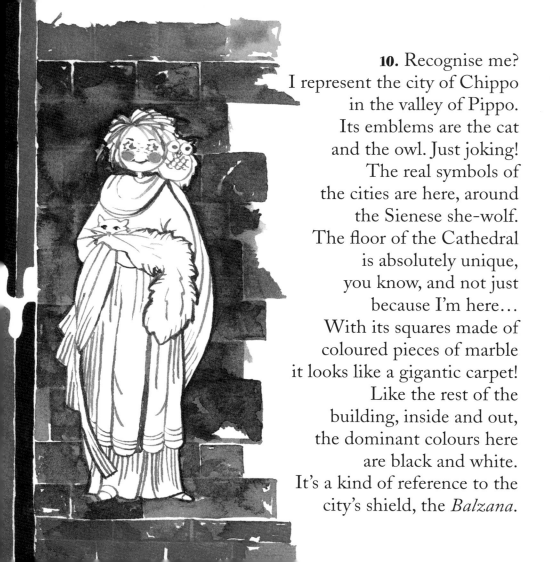

10. Recognise me? I represent the city of Chippo in the valley of Pippo. Its emblems are the cat and the owl. Just joking! The real symbols of the cities are here, around the Sienese she-wolf. The floor of the Cathedral is absolutely unique, you know, and not just because I'm here… With its squares made of coloured pieces of marble it looks like a gigantic carpet! Like the rest of the building, inside and out, the dominant colours here are black and white. It's a kind of reference to the city's shield, the *Balzana*.

11. Pope Pius II (Aeneas Silvius Piccolomini) was one of the Renaissance's most famous popes, and a great book collector. His nephew (also a pope) decided to turn his uncle's private library into a public one. He had a new room built inside the Cathedral and started filling it with books; but then he died, and the project was never completed. But you can always take a peek at the frescos telling the story of Pope Pius and at the splendid manuscripts belonging to the Cathedral and to the Spedale di Santa Maria della Scala.

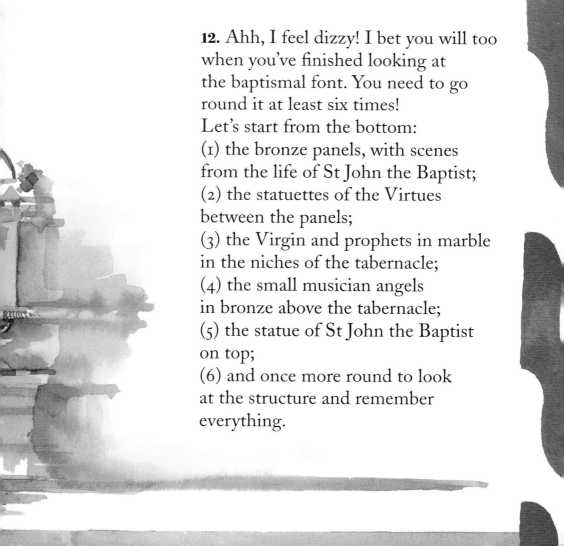

12. Ahh, I feel dizzy! I bet you will too when you've finished looking at the baptismal font. You need to go round it at least six times!
Let's start from the bottom:
(1) the bronze panels, with scenes from the life of St John the Baptist;
(2) the statuettes of the Virtues between the panels;
(3) the Virgin and prophets in marble in the niches of the tabernacle;
(4) the small musician angels in bronze above the tabernacle;
(5) the statue of St John the Baptist on top;
(6) and once more round to look at the structure and remember everything.

13. Siena, a city of painters…

14. The Virgin in this famous fresco
is surrounded by a full entourage.
But who are all these people?
It's not hard to recognise them,
because saints are depicted
in very precise ways. St Paul has
a long brown beard and a sword;
St Peter has a short, white,
curly beard and one or two keys;
St John the Evangelist is old,
bald, severe-looking, has a white
beard and is holding a book;
St John the Baptist is very thin,
has a ruffled beard and hair, and
is wearing a camel-hair tunic…
Spotted them? Want a tip?
Have a look at those people
propping up the canopy…

15. The Adoration of the Magi was a very popular theme with Sienese and other artists. Besides the religious significance, the episode provided a good excuse to paint exotic animals (seen the camel?) and magnificent original costumes. Not forgetting, of course, that the beautiful fabrics were good publicity for local artisans, especially the dyers and weavers.

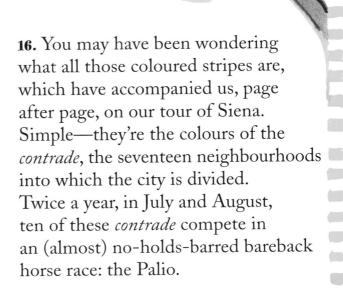

16. You may have been wondering what all those coloured stripes are, which have accompanied us, page after page, on our tour of Siena. Simple—they're the colours of the *contrade*, the seventeen neighbourhoods into which the city is divided. Twice a year, in July and August, ten of these *contrade* compete in an (almost) no-holds-barred bareback horse race: the Palio.

17. And now for a well-earned rest!

Unless, that is, you want a nice walk
in the Sienese countryside.
It's so harmonious even the cypresses
seem to have read
the treatises
on architecture…

What we've seen:

Giovanni di Turino,
The Sienese She-wolf.
Palazzo Pubblico.

Simone Martini,
Virgin Enthroned.
Palazzo Pubblico.

Simone Martini (attributed to),
Guidoriccio da Fogliano.
Palazzo Pubblico.

Ambrogio Lorenzetti,
The Effects of Good Government in the City.
Palazzo Pubblico.

Nicola and Giovanni Pisano,
pulpit.
Cathedral.

14th-century artist,
The Sienese She-wolf.
Cathedral floor.

Bernardino di Betto known as
Pinturicchio, *Stories of Pius II.*
Piccolomini Library.

Donatello, Jacopo della Quercia,
Lorenzo Ghiberti and other artists,
baptismal font. Baptistery.

Duccio di Buoninsegna,
Jesus before Annas,
St Peter Denying Jesus.
Opera del Duomo Museum.

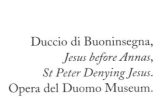

Domenico di Bartolo,
Ministering to the Sick and Injured.
Santa Maria della Scala,
Pilgrims' Hospice.

Domenico Beccafumi,
The Nativity of the Virgin.
Pinacoteca Nazionale.

Bartolo di Fredi,
The Adoration of the Magi.
Pinacoteca Nazionale.

Stefano di Giovanni di Consolo
known as Sassetta, *Epiphany.*
Chigi Saracini Collection (property
of the Monte dei Paschi di Siena).

Vincenzo Rustici,
Parade of the contrade.
Rocca Salimbeni
(Monte dei Paschi di Siena Collection).

... and the emblems

Balzana

1. *Leocorno*
Unicorn

2. *Torre*
Tower

3. *Tartuca*
Turtle

4. *Valdimontone*
Ram

5. *Nicchio*
Shell

6. *Chiocciola*
Snail

7. *Oca*
Goose

8. *Pantera*
Pantheress

9. *Giraffa*
Giraffe

10. *Civetta*
Owl

11. *Drago*
Dragon

12. *Onda*
Wave

13. *Istrice*
Porcupine

14. *Bruco*
Caterpillar

15. *Lupa*
She-wolf

16. *Selva*
Forest

17. *Aquila*
Eagle